Produced by the Statistics and Research Branch of the Northern Ireland Office.
For additional copies, please contact:

Statistics and Research Branch,
Criminal Justice Policy Division,
Massey House,
Stoney Road,
Belfast BT4 3SX

Telephone: 028 9052 7534   Fax: 028 9052 7532

Email: statistics.nio@nics.gov.uk

This publication is also available on the Internet at:
www.nio.gov.uk

First published 2003
Application for reproduction should be made to Statistics and Research Branch,
Massey House, Stoney Road, Belfast, BT4 3SX.

Foreword by the Secretary of State for Northern Ireland

Following the publication of Gender and the Northern Ireland Criminal Justice System , I am very pleased to be publishing the second in the series of publications in pursuance of my duties under Article 56 of the Criminal Justice (NI) Order 1996. Its aim is to provide statistical and research information to those involved in the administration of criminal justice, which will help them avoid discriminating against anyone on any improper ground. This will also assist organisations in fulfilling their duties under Section 75 of the Northern Ireland Act 1998.

This publication focuses on age and the Northern Ireland criminal justice system. I will be publishing further information on other topics in pursuance of my duties under this Article.

It is essential that practices and processes are — and are seen to be — properly followed and are informed by reliable statistical and research information. Those who have duties to perform in the administration of justice should find the data contained in this publication relevant and useful.

The Rt. Hon. Paul Murphy MP

Secretary of State for Northern Ireland

Northern Ireland Office

April 2003

Article 56
Criminal Justice (NI) Order 1996

1.   (1) The Secretary of State shall publish such information as he considers expedient for the purpose of —

        (a) enabling persons engaged in the administration of criminal justice to become aware of the financial implications of their decisions; or

        (b) facilitating the performance by such persons of their duty to avoid discriminating against any persons on any improper ground.

    (2) Publication under paragraph (1) shall be effected in such manner as the Secretary of State considers appropriate for the purpose of bringing the information to the attention of the persons concerned.

    (3) The Secretary of State may make rules regulating the collection of information under this Article.

Age and the Northern Ireland Criminal Justice System

OVERVIEW OF FINDINGS

Chapter

1

Key Statistics

Victims

- 4 out of 5 victims of violent crime are under 45 years old.

- By the age of 65 the risk of being a victim of crime reduces to 1%.

- 6% of households where the head of the household is aged 16-24 are burgled, compared to 1% where the head of the household is aged between 65 and 74.

- Almost half of victims of domestic violence are aged between 25 and 44.

Fear of crime

- Older people are more likely to feel unsafe out alone after dark whilst younger people are more likely to be fearful when home alone at night.

- Younger people are more likely than older people to feel very worried about being a victim of physical attack, racial or sectarian attack, rape and thefts of or from cars.

- Middle-aged people (45-59) are more likely to believe that they will be a victim of burglary or mugging/robbery.

Views on the Northern Ireland criminal justice system

- Whilst all age groups quote speeding as their top priority, people aged under 45 are more likely than older people to feel that illegal drug abuse should be the top priority for police in their local area. 45-59 year-olds are more likely to believe that burglary should be prioritised and the over 60 s are more likely to favour the prioritisation of drink-driving offences.

- Older people hold more favourable views of the police in terms of politeness, helpfulness, fairness and whether they do a good job.

- Younger people are more likely to feel that they understand the criminal justice system, to have confidence in its fairness and that judges are in-touch with ordinary people.

- The over 25 s are more likely to believe that court sentences should be stiffer but less likely than younger people to believe that a life sentence should be for the rest of a life.

Prosecutions

- The vast majority of persons prosecuted are under 40 years old; around one third are in their twenties and just under a quarter in their thirties.

- At 770 prosecutions per 10,000 population, the prosecution rate is highest for 18-20 year-olds.

- The majority of prosecutions brought against under 17 year-olds are for indictable offences. For older age groups the majority of prosecutions are for motoring offences.

Convictions

- Around three quarters of people convicted in court are aged between 18 and 39 years old.

- 6 out of 10 under 18 s convicted have committed indictable offences. For older age groups the majority of convictions are for motoring offences.

- 21-29 year-olds are more likely than other age groups to be convicted of violence against the person offences.

- Of people convicted of violent offences, the under 18 s are more likely than other age groups to be convicted of assaults occasioning actual bodily harm. Between the ages of 21 and 50, the most frequent conviction for a violent offence is for assaults on police.

- Of theft convictions, the over thirties are more likely to be convicted of shoplifting, whilst the under 21 s are the most likely of any age group to be convicted of taking a vehicle without the owner s consent.

- Of summary convictions, young people are more likely than older people to be convicted of public disorder offences.

Sentencing

- Young people under 18 convicted at court are much less likely to receive a fine than older people, but are more likely to be sentenced to community service, immediate custody or to be conditionally or absolutely discharged.
- Of people convicted of violent offences, those in their twenties and thirties are more frequently sentenced to immediate custody.
- The most likely groups to be sentenced to immediate custody are 18-20 year-olds and 21-29 year-olds convicted of acquisitive offences. The most likely group to be given community service is under 18 year-olds convicted of acquisitive offences.

Imprisonment

- On an average day in Northern Ireland prisons, around 350 prisoners are aged 21-29 years-old, 250 aged 30-39, 100 aged 40-49 and 50 aged 50-59 years old. 140 are under 21 and a little over 10 are aged 60 or over.

- Almost 9 out of 10 remand prisoners and almost 8 out of 10 sentenced prisoners are under 40 years old.

- Almost a quarter of prison receptions on sentence of immediate custody are under 21 years-old and almost 9 out of 10 are under 40 years-old. Almost two thirds received for fine default are under 30 years old and just over 8 out of 10 are under 40 years old.

VICTIMS

Chapter
2

Victims

Summary

In recent years the treatment and the rights of victims have gained priority in the criminal justice system. Legislation such as the Human Rights Act (1998), codes of practice and charters all give citizens greater powers to challenge their treatment. The Review of the criminal justice system in Northern Ireland (2000) pays particular attention to the needs of victims.

Both recorded crime statistics and crime survey findings demonstrate age differences in victimisation rates. Of recorded crimes of violence, 4 out of 5 victims are under 45 years old. The 2001 Northern Ireland Crime Survey estimates that 10% of people aged 16-24 were victims of violent crime between September 2000 and August 2001. The likelihood of being a victim declines with age, so that by the age of 65 the risk of being a victim reduces to 1%.

The overall chance of being a victim of burglary is 2%. This increases to 6% for households where the head of household is aged between 16 and 24. At 1%, the risk is lowest for households where the head of household is aged between 65 and 74.

Of vehicle-owning households surveyed, 7% had been victims of vehicle-related theft. Again, the highest risk, at 17%, was associated with households where the head of household was aged between 16 and 24. Households where the head of household was over 75 years old had the lowest risk, at 1%.

Police Service of Northern Ireland records of domestic violence incidents show that almost half (46%) of victims are aged between 25 and 44, although records of other crimes may contain hidden domestic violence incidents.

Victims of violent crime

- There were 29,757 victims of recorded violent crime (violence against the person, sexual offences, robbery) in 2001/02. Around 4 out of 5 were aged under 45 years and 2 out of 5 under 25 years.

- Of the 26,104 recorded offences against the person (murder, manslaughter and physical assaults), 8 out of 10 (81%) victims were aged under 45. Almost 3 out of 10 (29%) were aged 16-24 and over 1 in 10 (13%) were under 16 years old.

- 9 out of 10 victims of recorded sexual offences were aged under 45, with almost a quarter (24%) aged 16-24 and more than 2 out of 5 (44%) aged under 16.

- Almost one third (32%) of recorded victims of robbery were companies (or the age of the victim was unknown). Almost half (49%) were aged under 45, of which 17% were aged 16-24 and 4% under 16. Almost 1 in 5 (19%) was 45 or older, of which 6% were 65 or older.

Victims of violent crime in Northern Ireland 2001/02

Offences against the person

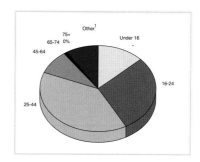

Sexual offences

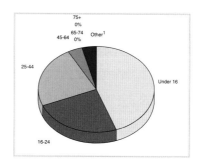

Robbery

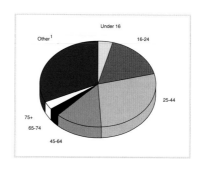

[1] Other includes private companies or where the age of the victim is not known

---

Source: Police Service of Northern Ireland, Central Statistics Unit

Victims and crime surveys

• As not all crimes are reported to the police, crime surveys are employed as a method of gathering information on crime victimisation to complement the information recorded by the police.

• 3,010 adults were interviewed in the Northern Ireland Crime Survey (2001). One fifth (20%) had been victims of crime between September 2000 and August 2001.

• 14% had been victimised once, 3% twice and 3% more than twice.

• 3% of respondents had been a victim of violent crime.

• The most likely victims of violent crime during 2000/01 were young people aged 16-24 (10%). Young men in this age group (17%) were much more likely to be victims than young women (5%).

Victims of violent crime

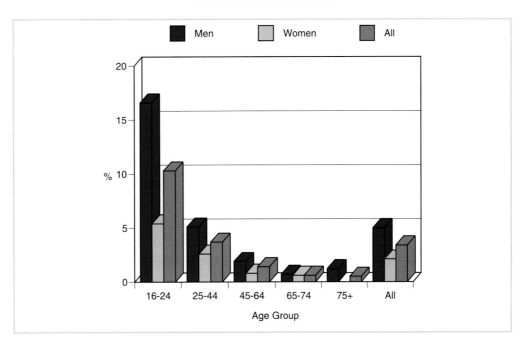

Source: Northern Ireland Crime Survey 2001. Data from NIO Statistics and Research Branch

Victims and crime surveys

- According to the Northern Ireland Crime Survey, the prevalence rate for burglary in 2000/01 was 2%. The households most likely to be victims of burglary contained heads of household aged 16-24 (6%).

- Households where the head of household was aged between 65 and 74 were least likely to be victims of burglary (1%)

- The overall risk of experiencing a vehicle-related theft in 2000/01 was 7%. The households most at risk were those containing heads of household aged 16-24 (17%). Those least at risk contained heads of household aged 75 years or above (1%).

Victims of burglary and vehicle related theft

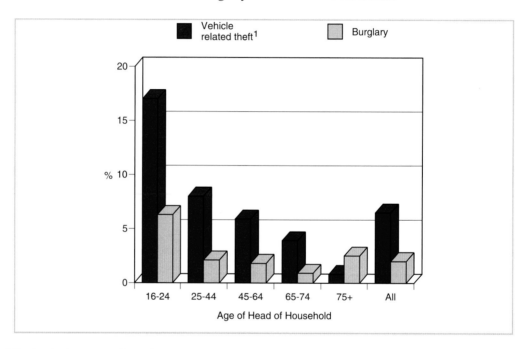

[1] % of vehicle-owning households

Source: Northern Ireland Crime Survey 2001. Data from NIO Statistics and Research Branch

Domestic violence

- In the financial year 2001/02 the Police Service of Northern Ireland attended 11,508 incidents of domestic violence. Around half of such incidents involved physical violence.

- The age of the victim was recorded in 8,832 (77%) cases.

- Of the total number of victims, 5,335 (46%) were aged between 25 and 44; 1,559 (14%) were aged between 16 and 24; and 1,577 (14%) were aged between 45 and 64.

- Whilst smaller proportions of victims were under 16 (2%) or over 65 years old (1%), this still represents 189 and 172 victims respectively.

Victims of domestic violence 2001/02

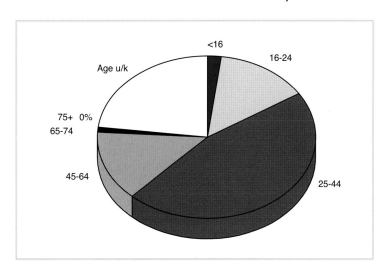

Source: Community Involvement Branch, Police Service of Northern Ireland

FEAR OF CRIME

Chapter 3

Fear of crime

Summary

Concern about becoming a victim of crime may be measured in several ways. The Northern Ireland Crime Survey looks at worry about specific crimes and feelings of safety when out alone or home alone after dark. The Community Attitudes Survey also asks respondents to state how likely they believe it is that they will become victims of specific crimes.

Some aspects of fear of crime seem to be age-related. In terms of personal safety, older people are more likely to feel unsafe out alone after dark whilst younger people are more likely to be fearful when home alone at night.

There are also differences in relation to fear of different types of crime. Age differences are most apparent in relation to worry about physical attack, racial or sectarian attack, rape, and thefts of or from cars. For all of these, younger people are more likely to feel very worried than older people. This fear is most acute amongst 16-29 year-olds.

Most people believe that crime is not very common in their local area. Where there is a perception of a high prevalence of crime, the likelihood of holding this perception declines with age.

Despite having a fear of crime, most people recognise the low risk of victimisation. Middle-aged people (45-59) are more likely to believe that they will be a victim of burglary or mugging/robbery. Young people (16-24) are more likely to believe that their house will be vandalised.

Feeling safe

- Older people are more likely to feel very unsafe walking alone in their local area after dark. Almost 1 in 5 people aged over 60 expressed this fear compared to around 1 in 10 in younger age groups.

- Women generally tend to feel more fearful about this than men, with older women most fearful. One quarter of women aged over 60 feel very unsafe compared to fewer than 1 in 10 men in the same age group.

- Generally, small proportions of crime survey respondents express feeling very unsafe at home alone at night (about 1% overall). Younger people are more likely to express this fear than older people are (2% of 16-29 year-olds compared to 1% in older age groups).

- Again, in this category women are more fearful than men, with 16-29 year-old women most likely to feel very unsafe (3%).

Fear out alone at night[1]

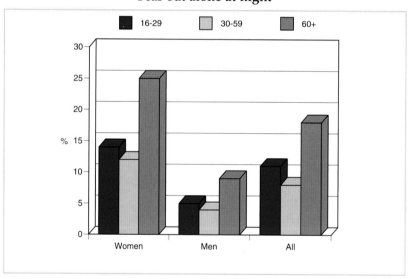

Fear home alone at night[1]

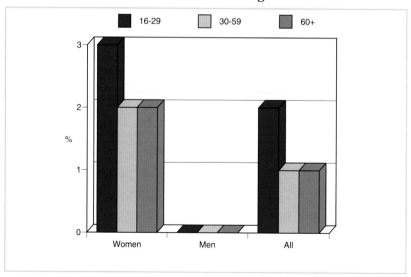

[1] Percentages feeling very unsafe

Source: Northern Ireland Crime Survey 2001. Data from NIO Statistics and Research Branch

Worry about crime

- The age of respondents has little effect on the likelihood of them being very worried about burglary (17-18% of all age groups responding to the Northern Ireland Crime Survey).

- For other crimes, such as physical attack (23% of 16-29 year-olds compared to 16% overall), race or sectarian attack (16% of 16-29 year-olds compared to 11% overall) and rape (24% of 16-29 year-olds compared to 16% overall), younger people are more likely to be very worried than older people are.

- Younger people are also more likely than older people to be very worried about thefts of (26% of 16-29 year-olds compared to 23% overall) or from cars (20% of 16-29 year-olds compared to 16% overall).

Worry about crime by type[1]

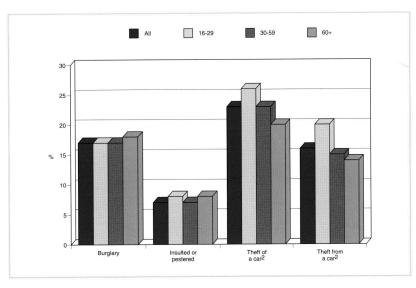

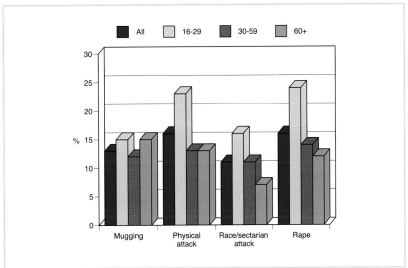

[1] Percentages saying they are very worried
[2] Based on vehicle owners only

Source: Northern Ireland Crime Survey 2001. Data from NIO Statistics and Research Branch

Perceptions of crime in local area

- Generally, less than one third of respondents to the Community Attitudes Survey (CAS) in 2000 believed crimes to be common in their local area. However, within that proportion, younger people were more likely to perceive crimes to be very or fairly common in their local area.

- For some crime categories the perception of prevalence, whilst being low overall, declines with age. People aged 16-24 were most likely to believe mugging to be common in their area (6%) compared to 1% of over 75s.

- More than one quarter (27%) of 16-24 year-olds believed drug abuse to be common compared to around one tenth (11%) of over 75s.

- People in the 45-59 age group were most likely to perceive burglary or car theft as being common and people aged under 45 are most likely to perceive vandalism as being common.

Perceived regularity of crime in local area[1]

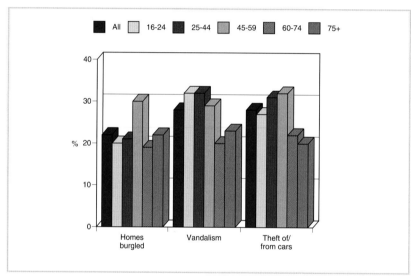

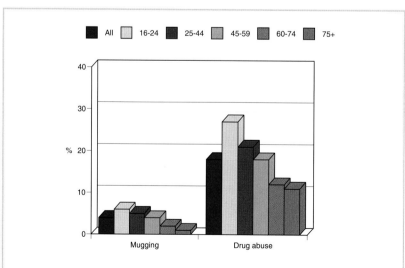

[1] Percentages saying each crime type is very/fairly common

Source: Community Attitudes Survey 2000. Data from NIO Statistics and Research Branch

Perceived likelihood of victimisation

• Despite having a fear of crime, most people recognise that the chances of being a victim of crime are low. Generally, less than one third of all respondents to the Community Attitudes Survey 2000 believed it to be very or fairly likely that they would be victimised.

• Regarding burglary (24%) and mugging / robbery (9%) people aged 45-59 were most likely to believe that they might be victimised. People aged 16-24 (18%) were most likely to believe that their home would be vandalised.

• People in the youngest and oldest age groups did not believe that they would be a victim of car crime. This partly reflects the lower number of car owners in these age groups.

Likelihood of victimisation by type of crime[1]

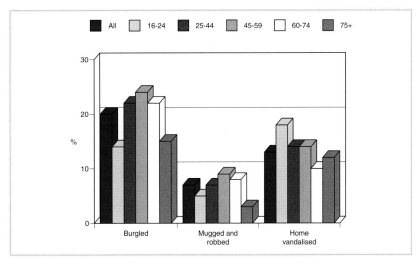

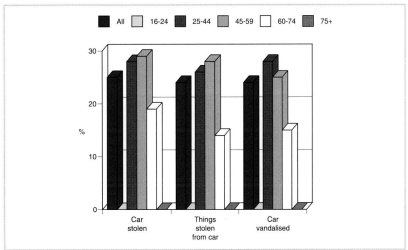

[1] Respondents stating that victimisation was very or fairly likely

Source: Community Attitudes Survey 2000. Data from NIO Statistics and Research Branch

Perceived problems in local neighbourhood

- Younger crime survey respondents are more likely than older respondents are to identify anti-social behaviours or poor social conditions as problems in their local area.

- Almost double the proportion of 16-29 year-olds (43%) as people aged 60 or over (24%) stated that vandalism, graffiti or other deliberate damage to property was a problem.

- A similar proportion of 16-29 year-olds (43%) stated that teenagers hanging around on the streets was a problem. Again, this compares with a much lower proportion of people aged 60 and over (26%).

- For all categories listed, the propensity to perceive the presence of problems declined with age.

Perceived problems in local neighbourhood[1]

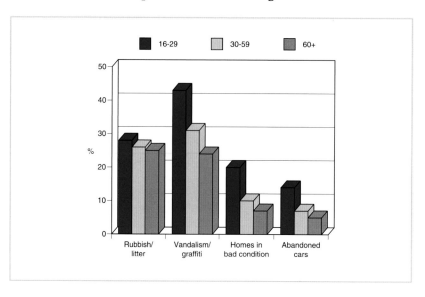

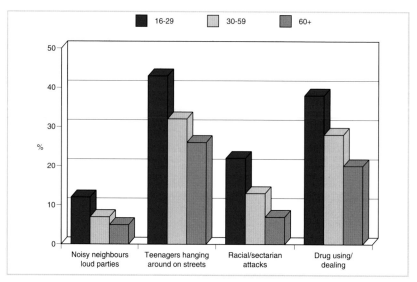

[1] Percentages saying 'very big' or 'fairly big' problem

Source: Northern Ireland Crime Survey 2001. Data from NIO Statistics and Research Branch

VIEWS ON THE NORTHERN IRELAND CRIMINAL JUSTICE SYSTEM

Chapter 4

Views on the Northern Ireland criminal justice system

Summary

Older people tend to estimate a greater increase in crime in Northern Ireland over the previous two years than younger people. Whilst speeding is the most frequently quoted preference for top priority for police in their local area, the under 45s are more likely than older people to favour the prioritisation of illegal drug abuse, 45-59 year-olds are more likely than other age groups to prefer burglary to be prioritised and the over 60s are more likely than younger people to believe that the police should prioritise drink driving.

Older people are more likely to rate the police more positively in terms of politeness and helpfulness. They are also more likely to believe that the police deal fairly with everyone and do a good job.

Younger people are more likely to feel that they understand the way in which courts work, to have confidence in the fairness of the criminal justice system and to believe that judges are in touch with what ordinary people think.

Whilst people aged over 25 are more likely to believe that court sentences should be stiffer, they are less likely than younger people to believe that a life sentence should be for the rest of a life.

Perceptions of crime

- When asked about changes in the level of crime in Northern Ireland over the last two years, older people tend to estimate a greater increase than younger people.

- More than half (56%) of people aged 65 and over believed there to be a lot more crime compared to two years ago. This compares to under a third (29%) of 16-24 year-olds.

Perceptions of change in the level of crime in Northern Ireland over past two years.

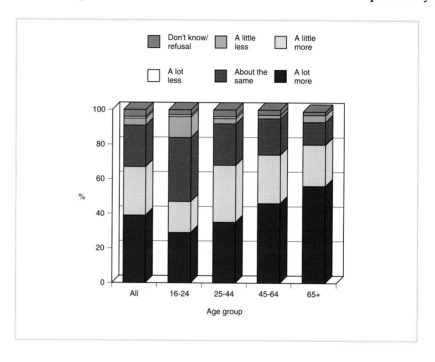

Source: Review of the Criminal Justice System in Northern Ireland 2000, Research Report 1: Attitudes to Crime, Crime Reduction and Community Safety in Northern Ireland

Views on local policing priorities

- When asked what type of crime should receive most attention from police in their own area, the responses of all age groups were quite similarly distributed.

- While the most frequent response overall was speeding , almost half of the over 60s (43%) stated this, compared to one fifth (20%) of 16-24 year-olds.

- The second most frequent response of the under 45s was illegal drug abuse (10% of 16-24 year-olds and 14% of 25-44 year-olds). This was ranked joint third (with vandalism) by 45-59 year-olds (12%) and joint fourth (with drink driving) by the over 60s (10%)

- Damage to property / vandalism was the third preference of 16-24 year-olds (13%), 25-44 year-olds (13% - joint with burglary) and 45-59 year-olds (12% - joint with illegal drug abuse).

What should receive most attention from police locally?

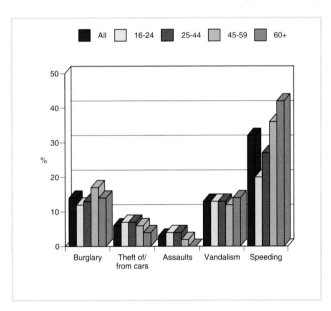

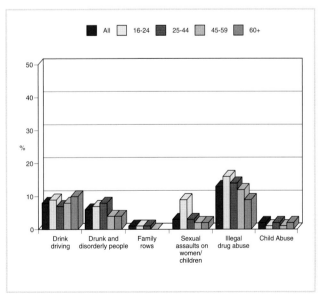

Source: Community Attitudes Survey 2000. Data from NIO Statistics and Research Branch

Views on policing prioritisation in Northern Ireland

- When asked which type of crime should receive most attention from police on a Northern Ireland basis all age groups differed from their responses to local policing issues.

- Again, the distribution of responses was similar across age groups, with a majority of all age groups believing that illegal drug abuse should be prioritised.

- Younger respondents were more likely to mention assaults as a priority (16% of 16-24 year-olds and 10% of 25-44 year-olds compared to 5% each of 45-59 year-olds and the over 60s).

- Respondents aged 45-59 were more likely to mention damage to property (8%) and the over 60s more likely to mention burglary (8%).

What should receive most attention from police in Northern Ireland?

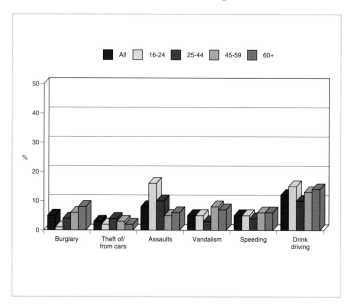

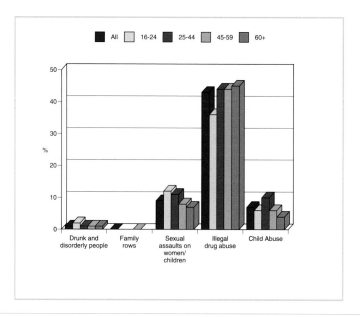

Source: Community Attitudes Survey 2000. Data from NIO Statistics and Research Branch

Views on the police

- Older people are more likely to rate the police more positively in terms of politeness and helpfulness. This difference is particularly pronounced for those rating the police as very polite or very helpful.

- Almost half (45%) of 60 —74 year-olds and half (50%) of the over 75s rate the police in their area as very polite. This is around double the proportions of 16-24 year-olds (20%) and 25-44 year-olds (26%).

- Again almost half (44%) of 60-74 year-olds and the over 75s (46%) rate the police as very helpful, compared to lower proportions of 16-24 year-olds (16%) and 25-44 year-olds (24%).

Ratings of politeness and helpfulness of police.

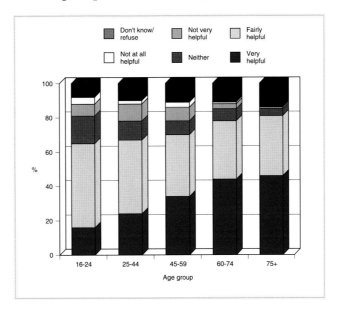

Helpfulness

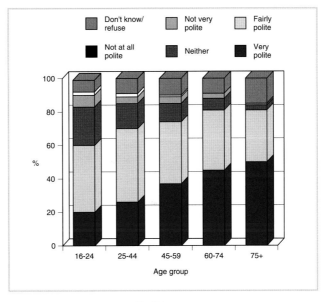

Politeness

Source: Community Attitudes Survey 2000. Data from NIO Statistics and Research Branch

Perceptions of police

- Younger people are less likely to believe that when dealing with ordinary (non-terrorist) crime the police deal fairly with everyone. The likelihood of holding this view increases with age.

- Older people are more likely to believe that the police in their area do a very good job, over one third (36%) of the over 75s believed this, compared to 15% of 16-24 year-olds).

- This difference is less apparent for respondents who believed the police to be doing a fairly good job. More than half of 16-24 year-olds (52%) and 25-44 year-olds (51%) believed this. The proportions of older people believing this was offset by the proportions believing the police to do a very good job.

Views on the fairness and effectiveness of police

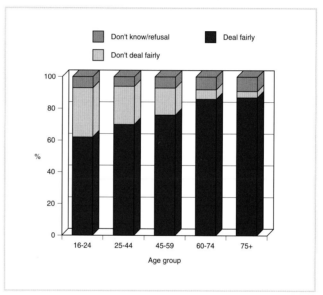

Fairness

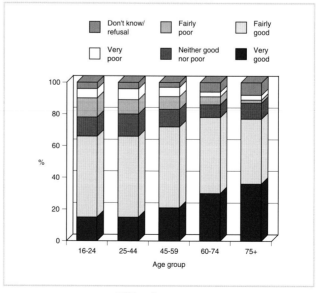

Effectiveness

Source: Community Attitudes Survey 2000. Data from NIO Statistics and Research Branch

Confidence in the criminal justice system

- Whilst under half of respondents aged 25-44 (46%) and 45-59 (43%) feel that they understand the way in which courts work, these are higher proportions than for other age groups.

- People aged over 75 (24%) are least likely to express an understanding of how courts work.

- 7 out of 10 people aged 16-24 and 25-44 stated that they were very or fairly confident in the fairness of the criminal justice system. People aged 45-59 (65%) and over 75 (62%) were less inclined to say this.

Awareness of and confidence in the criminal justice system in Northern Ireland

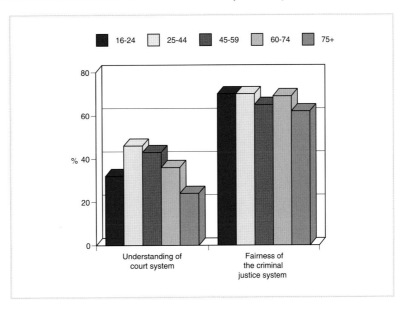

Source: Community Attitudes Survey 2000. Data from NIO Statistics and Research Branch

The Judiciary

- Young people aged 16-24 (35%) are most likely to believe that judges are in touch with what ordinary people think. Around one fifth of 25-44 year olds (22%) and those aged 65 and over (22%) agreed.

- People aged 25-44 (70%) are most likely to believe that the judiciary is out of touch . This includes more than one third (37%) of this age group who believed that the judiciary is very out of touch .

Views on whether the Judiciary is in touch with what ordinary people think

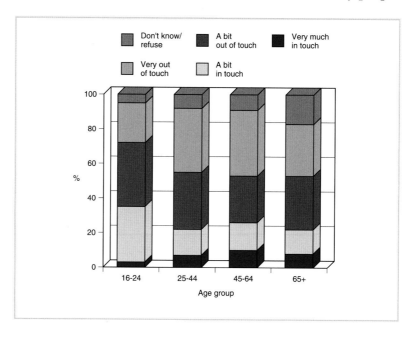

Source: Review of the Criminal Justice System in Northern Ireland 2000, Research Report 2:
           Attitudes to the Criminal Justice System in Northern Ireland

Sentencing

• Regarding ordinary crime (where there is no sectarian or terrorist involvement), young people aged 16-24 were more inclined than other age groups to believe that sentences handed out by the courts were about right . Most people in other age groups believed they should be stiffer.

• Almost half of 16-24 year-olds (49%) felt that a life sentence should be for the rest of a life. The likelihood of holding this view declined with age.

• Where sectarian/terrorist crime is concerned, around two thirds of all age groups surveyed thought that sentences should be stiffer. Around half of all age groups felt that a life sentence for this type of crime should mean life.

Views on sentencing non-sectarian/terrorist crime in Northern Ireland

Severity of sentences

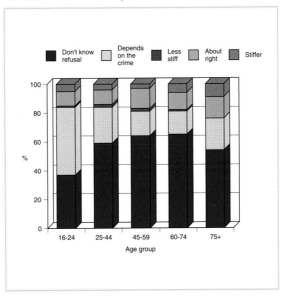

Extent of a life sentence ('ordinary crime')

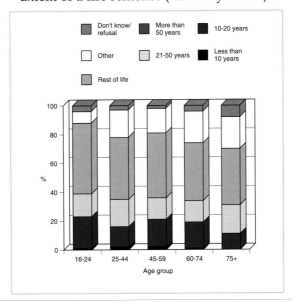

Source: Community Attitudes Survey 2000. Data from NIO Statistics and Research Branch

Sentencing

- When estimating the proportions of offenders (burglars, muggers and rapists) that are sent to prison, young people aged 16-24 tend to make higher estimates than older people.

- Whilst younger people believe that more offenders are sent to prison, when estimating the proportions that <u>should</u> be sent, older people generally hold stronger views.

- Views on preferred imprisonment rates for burglars and muggers show some degree of variation across age groups. However, views on the preferred rate for rapists are more closely aligned, with 25-44 year-olds in particular believing that virtually all rapists should be imprisoned.

**Estimates of proportions of offenders sent to prison
and proportions that should be sent**

Burglars

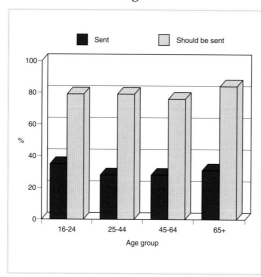

Muggers

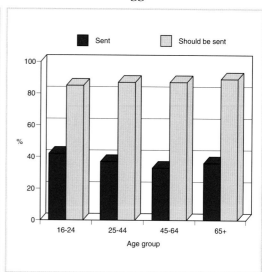

Rapists

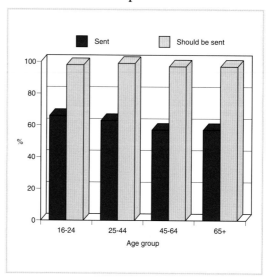

Source: Review of the Criminal Justice System in Northern Ireland 2000, Research Report 1:
Attitudes to Crime, Crime Reduction and Community Safety in Northern Ireland

PROSECUTIONS

Chapter 5

Prosecutions

Summary

The vast majority of persons prosecuted are under 40 years old; around a third are in their twenties and just under a quarter in their thirties. When standardised according to population size, the prosecution rate is highest for 18-20 year-olds, at 770 prosecutions per 10,000 population. These trends are apparent at both Crown and magistrates courts levels.

Trends in prosecutions for different age groups are largely similar and there is little annual variation in the age distribution of the offender population. However, a small but steady decline in the numbers of 21-29 year-olds prosecuted has been offset by a corresponding increase in prosecutions of 18-20 year-olds. Whilst the annual number of prosecutions has been falling in general, the rate of decline for 21-29 year-olds has been greater than for other age groups.

With regard to types of crime, the majority of prosecutions brought against under 17s are for indictable[1] offences. For older age groups the majority of prosecutions are for motoring offences. Under 17 year-olds are less likely to plead not guilty at court and slightly higher proportions are found not guilty.

[1]Throughout this chapter, references to indictable offences include those dealt with at both Crown and magistrates courts

All court prosecutions in Northern Ireland 1999

- In 1999 there was a total of 30,439 prosecutions[1] carried out at the Crown Court and magistrates courts. Of this total number, over one third (35%) were aged between 21-29 years and almost one quarter (23%) were aged 30-39 years.

- Defendants aged between 18 and 39 years accounted for over three quarters (76%) of those prosecuted in Northern Ireland in 1999. Meanwhile 6% (1,881) of all prosecutions, were of defendants aged under 18.

- When standardised according to population size, the 18-20 year-old age group has the highest prosecution rate, at 770 per 10,000 population. Over the age of 18, this rate declines with age, reaching 42 prosecutions per 10,000 population for the over 50s.

All court prosecutions in Northern Ireland 1999

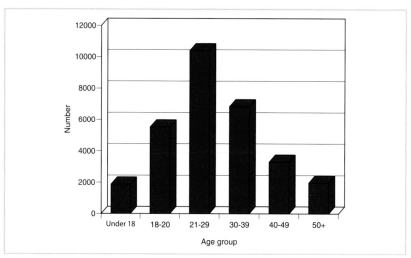

All court prosecutions in Northern Ireland per 10,000 population 1999

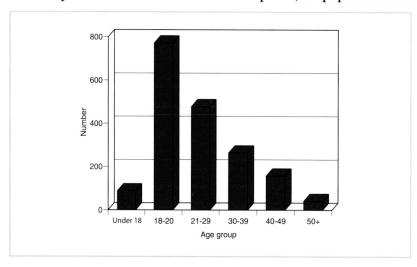

[1] Includes 500 defendants for whom no age was recorded

Source: NIO Statistics and Research Branch

All court prosecutions in Northern Ireland 1995-1999

- The age group 21-29 constitutes the largest proportion (over one third) of all annual court prosecutions in Northern Ireland, through the period 1995 to 1999.

- In contrast, those in the age groups 17 and under, and 50+ represent the smallest proportion (between 6-7% each) of annual court prosecutions between 1995-1999.

- There is little annual variation in the proportions of age groups comprising all court prosecutions (1995-1999). However, there has been a small but steady decline in the proportion of prosecutions within the age group 21-29 (38% in 1995 falling to 35% in 1999), and a converse rise within the age group 18-20 (16% in 1995 to 19% in 1999).

All court prosecutions in Northern Ireland 1995-1999

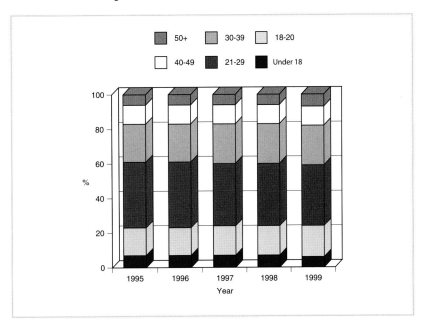

Source: NIO Statistics and Research Branch

Crown Court and magistrates' court prosecutions 1999

- The age distribution of defendants prosecuted at Crown and magistrates courts in 1999 is similar.

- In 1999, 18-39 year-olds accounted for over three-quarters (78%) of all 853[1] Crown Court prosecutions, of which 37% were aged 21-29 years.

- Much smaller proportions of defendants were aged 17 years or less (6%) or over 50 years (6%).

- This pattern was also evident in the 29,084[2] magistrates courts prosecutions in 1999, of which 18-39 year-olds comprised 76% of the total. The largest proportion of these prosecutions was within the age group 21-29 years (35%).

Crown Court prosecutions in Northern Ireland 1999

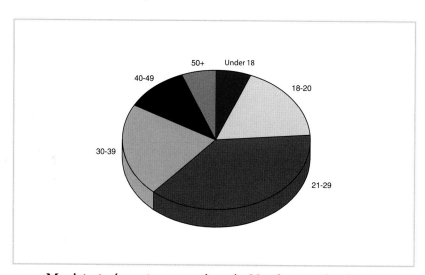

Magistrates' court prosecutions in Northern Ireland 1999

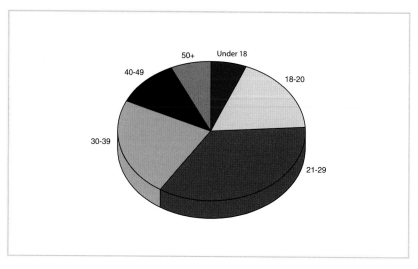

[1] Excludes 4 defendants for whom no age was recorded
[2] Excludes 498 defendants for whom no age was recorded

Source: NIO Statistics and Research Branch

All court prosecutions in Northern Ireland by offence classification 1999

- The majority of prosecutions (60%) of individuals up to the age of 17 were for indictable offences. In contrast, prosecutions within all other age groups were mainly for motoring offences.

- The frequency of a defendant being prosecuted for an indictable offence decreases with age, from 60% of the under 18s to 16% of the over 50s.

- Conversely, the chance of a prosecution being for a motoring offence increases with age, from 21% of under 18s to 70% of the over 50s.

- Summary offences remain the lowest proportion of all prosecutions regardless of age, representing no more than one fifth (20%) of any age group.

All court prosecutions in Northern Ireland by offence classification 1999

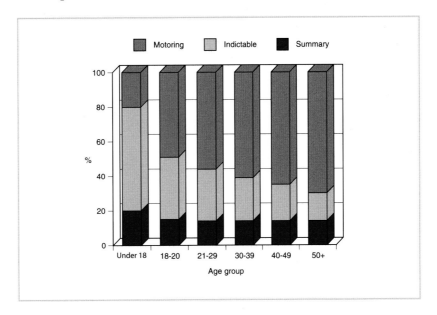

Source: NIO Statistics and Research Branch

All court prosecutions for indictable offences 1995-1999

- In 1999 indictable offences represented almost one third (30%) of all court prosecutions in Northern Ireland.

- Most defendants prosecuted for indictable offences over the period 1995 to 1999 were found in the age group 21-29, whilst much lower numbers were aged 50 and over.

- Between the years 1995 to 1999, there was an overall decrease in the number of indictable prosecutions in all courts in Northern Ireland for every age group. This drop was greatest within the 21-29 age group, where numbers fell by over one quarter (26%) from 4,146 to 3,071. The age range 30-39 experienced a similar decrease (24%), from 2,211 in 1995 to 1,685 in 1999.

- Between 1998 and 1999 the number of prosecutions in the age group 18-20 increased by 6%. In contrast all other age groups continued the downward trend, with numbers dropping by between 2% (age range 40-49) and 16% (under 18 year-olds).

Indictable prosecutions at all courts 1995-1999

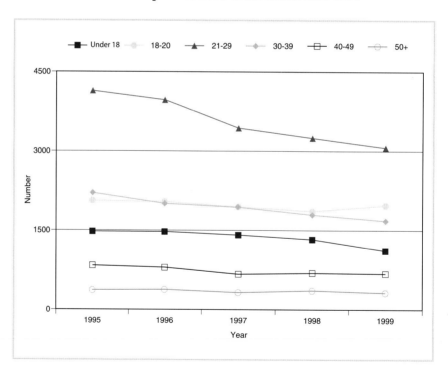

Source: NIO Statistics and Research Branch

All court prosecutions for summary offences 1995-1999

- In 1999 summary offences accounted for 14% of all court prosecutions in Northern Ireland.

- The 21-29 age group had the greatest number of annual summary prosecutions, while defendants aged 50 and over accounted for the least.

- Since 1995 summary prosecutions of defendants aged 21-29 decreased by the greatest proportion (23%) of all the age groups.

- Between 1998 and 1999 summary prosecutions rose by one fifth (20%) within the 50+ age bracket, while all other age groups experienced a decrease in such prosecutions, by between 8% (18-20 and 40-49 years) and 23% (under 18 s).

Summary prosecutions at all courts 1995-1999

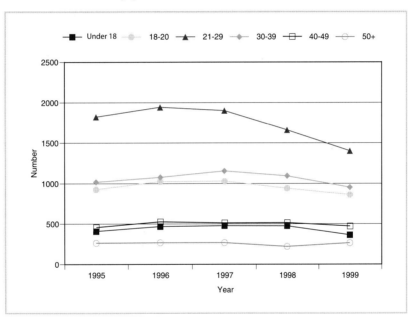

All court prosecutions for motoring offences 1995-1999

- In 1999 motoring offences accounted for over half (56%) of all court prosecutions in Northern Ireland.

- The largest number of motoring prosecutions in each of the years 1995 to 1999 were of 21-29 year-olds, followed by 30-39 year-olds. In contrast the least number of motoring prosecutions were found in the age range 17 and under.

- From 1995 to 1999 motoring prosecutions in the age group 21-29 fell by 22%. A fall of a lesser extent (11%) was also apparent within the age group 30-39 years where prosecutions dropped from 4,744 (1995) to 4,199 (1999).

- Between 1998 and 1999 the number of prosecutions increased for all ages above 17 years. This increase ranged from 1% (21-29 years) to 9% (18-20 year-olds). Prosecutions of young people up to 17 years of age decreased slightly during this period (<0.5%).

Motoring prosecutions at all courts 1995-1999

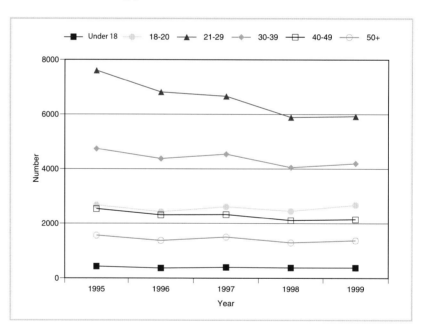

Source: NIO Statistics and Research Branch

Pleas and outcomes at all courts 1999

- In 1999 almost 9 out of 10 (88%) defendants pleaded guilty in Northern Ireland courts. This ranged from 83% to 88% of all age groups. An overall total of 12% of defendants pleaded not guilty in all courts.

- The percentage of defendants who were acquitted was greatest for the under 18s (15%). Throughout other age groups the acquittal rate was between 11% and 12%.

- The percentage of defendants who pleaded not guilty but were subsequently convicted varied little according to age group, representing only 1% of each age group over 18 years and 2% of under 18s.

Pleas and outcomes at all courts in Northern Ireland 1999

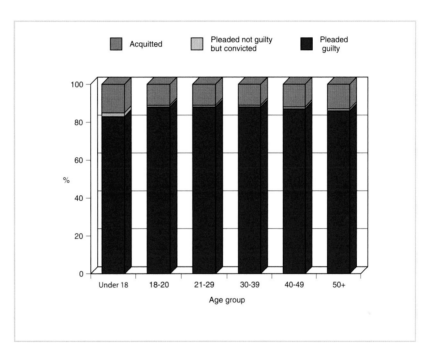

Source: NIO Statistics and Research Branch

CONVICTIONS

Chapter 6

Convictions

Summary

Around three quarters of people convicted in court are aged between 18 and 39 years old; about a fifth are aged 18-20, over a third aged 21-29 and almost a quarter are 30-39 years old. Six out of ten of the under 18s are convicted of indictable offences. For older age groups the majority of convictions are for motoring offences.

For most age groups the most common convictions for indictable offences are for theft. However, for 21-29 year-olds the most common is offences of violence against the person, accounting for more than a quarter of such convictions.

Within the specific category of violence, under 18s are more likely to be convicted of assaults occasioning actual bodily harm than for other violent offences. Between the ages of 21 and 50 the most frequent conviction for a violent offence is for assaults on police.

Of theft convictions, the over 30s are more likely to be convicted of shoplifting than of other theft offences. The under 21s are more likely than other age groups to be convicted of taking a vehicle without the owner s consent, which accounts for a quarter of theft convictions of 18-20 year-olds and a fifth of the under 18s.

Of summary convictions, younger people are more likely than older people to be convicted of public disorder offences. These account for almost two thirds of convictions for summary offences of 18-20 year-olds and more than half of 21-29 year-olds, compared to a fifth of the over fifties.

4 out of 10 motoring convictions of the under 18s are for driving without insurance, decreasing with age to 1 out of 10 of the over fifties. Older drivers are more likely to be convicted of driving with excess speed.

All court convictions by offence classification 1999

- The majority of people convicted in court are aged 18-39 - 76% (19,979), in 1999. Within this category 18% (4,858) were 18-20 year-olds, 35% (9,146) were 21-29 year-olds and 23% (5,976) were 30-39 year-olds.

- Across the three offence classifications of indictable, summary and motoring offences there are noticeable patterns across the age bands.

- As age increases the proportion convicted of motoring offences steadily increases - from 22% (356) of under 18s to 73% (1,250) of over 50s.

- In 1999 59% (937) of under 18s were convicted of indictable offences; however, the proportions steadily decrease with age to 14% (247) of over 50s.

- The proportions convicted of summary offences are similar over all the age bands and make up the lowest of the offence classifications.

All court convictions in Northern Ireland by offence classification 1999

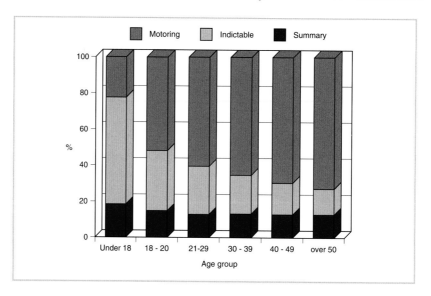

All court convictions for indictable offences 1999

- In 1999 the highest proportion of convictions for indictable offences within most of the age bands was for theft, particularly for under 18s (36%) and over 50s (39%). (The exception is 21-29 year-olds, where the highest proportion was for violence against the person (27%)).

- The second highest proportion of convictions within most of the age bands was for offences of violence against the person. The proportions increase up to the age group 21-29 (27%) and 30-39 (27%) and then steadily reduce to 20% of over 50s.

- The proportion convicted of sexual offences is less than 1% of 18-30 year-olds, increasing to 2% of 30-39 year-olds, 3% of 40-49 year-olds and steeply increasing to 10% of over 50s.

- The proportion of each age group convicted of burglary decreases steadily with increase in age from 19% of under 18s to 4% of over 50s.

- The proportion of each age group convicted of robbery is considerably less than for burglary and remains the same for all ages up to 39 years old (2%) decreasing to 1% of 40-49 year-olds and less than 1% of over 50s.

- The proportion of each age group convicted of fraud and forgery increases from 2% of under 18s and 6% of 18-20 year-olds to peak at 9% of 30-39 year-olds and then decreases gradually to 7% of over 50s.

Distribution of convictions for indictable offences 1999

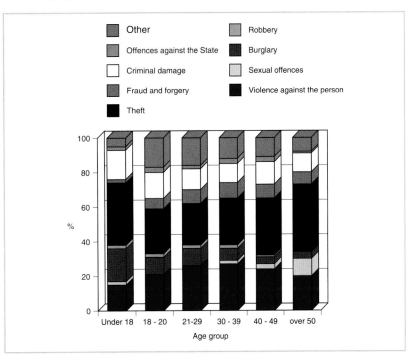

All court convictions for violence against the person offences 1999

- In 1999 the three main violence against the person offences that all ages were convicted of were: assault on police (32%), assault occasioning actual bodily harm (26%) and obstructing or resisting police (22%).

- The proportions of age groups convicted of assault on police rose from 22% (32) of under 18s to 40% of those aged 40-49 and then fell to 29% (14) of those over 50.

- Under 18s had the highest proportion (39%) of convictions of assault occasioning actual bodily harm. The proportions for other age groups were less, ranging from 23% of 21-29 year-olds to 29% of over 50s.

- Those aged 30-39 (19%) and 40-49 (17%) were less likely to be convicted of obstructing or resisting police. Under 21s had the highest proportion - 25% and 27% of under 18s and 18-20s respectively.

Distribution of offences for violence against the person convictions 1999

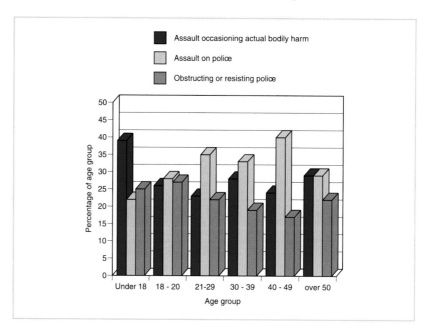

Source: NIO Statistics and Research Branch

50

All court convictions for theft offences 1999

- In 1999 only 3% of convictions of under 18 year-olds were for shoplifting. This rose steadily from 23% of 18-20 year-olds to 53% of over 50s.

- Higher proportions of under 21s were convicted of taking a vehicle without the owner s consent — 26% of 18-20 year-olds convicted and 22% of under 18s. The proportion dropped to 15% of 21-29 year-olds, 2% of 30-39 year-olds, 2% of 40-49 year-olds and 1% of the over 50s.

- The proportion convicted of handling stolen goods increased from 6% of the under 18s to 10% of 40-49 year-olds and fell to 5% of those over 50.

- Those aged 21-29 had the highest proportion of convictions for theft (40%) compared to 31% of under 18s and 33% of over 50s.

Distribution of offences for theft convictions 1999

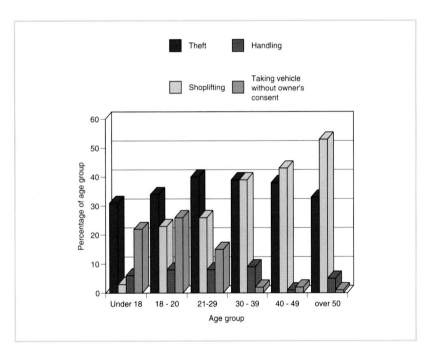

Source: NIO Statistics and Research Branch

All court convictions for summary offences 1999

- In 1999 the proportion of those convicted of public disorder offences was considerably larger for the 18-20 years olds (61%) and 21-29 year-olds (53%) than for other age groups, particularly over 50s (21%).

- As age increases, the proportion of those convicted of liquor licence offences also increases, from 2% (7) of under 18s to 26% (58) of over 50s.

- Those aged 40 and over tended to be convicted for a wide variety of summary offences.

Distribution of convictions for summary offences 1999

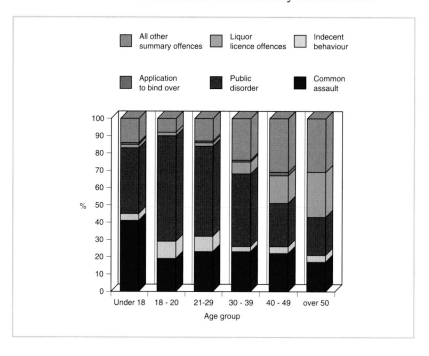

Source: NIO Statistics and Research Branch

All court convictions for motoring offences 1999

- In 1999 the proportion of those convicted of driving without insurance fell steadily with increase in age, from 41% (147) of under 18s to 10% (126) of over 50s.

- The proportion of each age group convicted of regulatory offences gradually increased with increase in age, from 2% (6) of under 18s to 9% and 8% of 40-49 year-olds and over 50s respectively.

- The proportion of under 18s convicted of driving whilst unfit was less than 1% compared to 3% - 4% of all other age groups.

All court convictions for motoring offences 1999

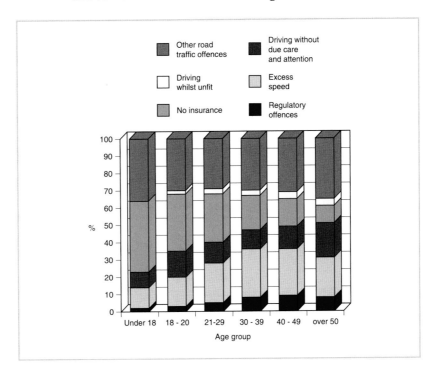

Source: NIO Statistics and Research Branch

Reconviction

- Reconviction rates are calculated on the basis of an individual being reconvicted within two years of an original conviction (or discharge from custody, if applicable) for an offence committed after the original conviction.

- Of adults convicted and given non-custodial sentences (e.g. probation, community service order), the reconviction rate decreases steadily with increase in age.

- The rate for 17-19 year-olds is almost three times that for 50-59 year-olds and five times the rate for the over 60s.

Reconviction rates for persons given non-custodial sentences

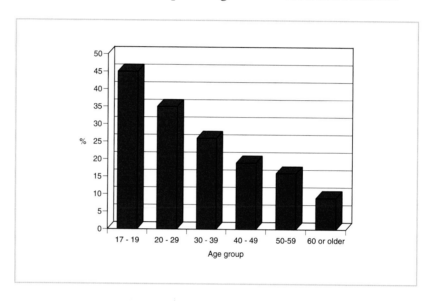

Source: Adult Reconviction in Northern Ireland. NIO Research and Statistical Bulletin 3/2000

SENTENCING

Sentencing

Summary

The use of the fine dominates sentencing in Northern Ireland courts. Overall, more than two thirds of convicted offenders are fined. However, young people under 18 are much less likely to receive a fine than older people but are more likely to be sentenced to community service or immediate custody or to be given a conditional or absolute discharge.

After a fine, the most frequent sentence given to convicted violent offenders is immediate custody. Whilst a quarter overall of these offenders are given this sentence, it is more frequently given to people in their twenties and thirties.

For summary offences the most frequent sentence after a fine is recognizance. People aged 18-20 within this category are most likely to be given this sentence.

The most likely groups to be sentenced to immediate custody are 18-20 year-olds and 21-29 year-olds convicted of acquisitive offences; more than a quarter of each of these groups is thus sentenced. The most likely group to be given community service is the under 18 group convicted of acquisitive offences, of whom more than 4 out of 10 are sentenced in this way.

All court disposals for all offences 1999

- The use of the fine dominates sentencing in Northern Ireland courts. Overall, 68% of all convicted offenders were fined in 1999. Under 18s were less likely to be fined (31%) compared to older age groups. The proportion more than doubled for 18-20 year-olds (65%) and gradually increased to 78% of 40-49 year-olds and 77% of over 50s.

- Of all age groups, those most likely to be given immediate custody, which includes being sent to a young offenders centre (YOC), juvenile justice centre or prison, were the under 18s (11%). The proportions decrease with increase in age, with only 3% (49) of over 50s being given immediate custody.

- Offenders aged under 18 are considerably more likely to be given community service (27%) than any other age group. The likelihood of receiving this sentence decreases with age from 9% of 18-20 year-olds to 2% of over 50s.

- The proportion of under 18s given a conditional or absolute discharge (22%) is more than three times that for any of the age groups aged between 18 and 49 (5-6%) and double that for those over 50 (10%).

Disposals for all offences at all courts 1999

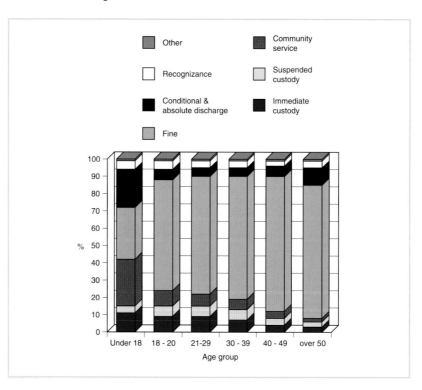

Source: NIO Statistics and Research Branch

All court disposals for indictable offences 1999

● Whilst a fine is the most frequently given sentence for indictable offences, the likelihood of receiving this sentence is less than it is for summary or motoring offences. In 1999 under 18s convicted of indictable offences were less likely to be given a fine (14%) than other age groups, the proportions of which ranged from 27% of 30-39 year-olds to 34% of over 50s.

● In 1999 the proportion of offenders under 18 given community service (36%) was considerably higher than for any other age group. The proportion steadily decreased from 21% (336) of 18-20 year-olds to 9% (23) of over 50s.

● The youngest and oldest age groups were more likely than middle age groups to be given a conditional or absolute discharge — 25% of under 18s and 22% of over 50s. The other age groups were about half as likely to be conditionally or absolutely discharged—from 10% of 18-20 and 21-29 year-olds to 14% of 40-49 year-olds.

● 21-29 year-olds convicted of indictable offences are the most likely to be given immediate custody (24%) and the youngest and oldest offenders are the least likely — 16% of under 18s and 15% of over 50s.

Distribution of disposals for indictable offences 1999

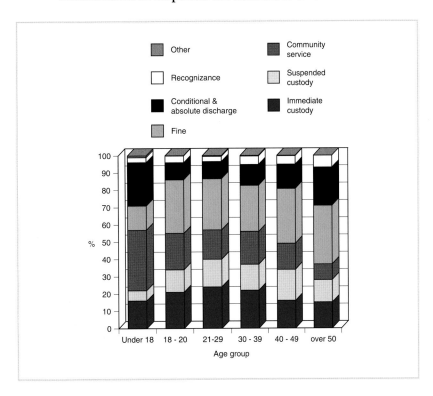

Source: NIO Statistics and Research Branch

All court disposals for violent offences[1] 1999

- The percentage of all convicted violent offenders given immediate custody in 1999 (25%) was nearly as high as the percentage given fines (27%).

- The proportion of each age group given immediate custody peaked at 27% of both 21-29 year-olds and 30-39 year-olds. This fell to 22% of under 18s and 23% of over 50s.

- The proportion of under 18s fined (18%) was considerably smaller than the proportions of other age groups, which ranged from 23% of 30-39 year-olds to 31% of over 50s.

- Under 18s were more likely to receive community service (33%) than the older age groups which ranged from 7% of the over 50s to 17% of 20-29 year-olds.

- The proportion of under 18s given suspended custody (7%) was half that for 18-20 year-olds (14%) whilst the proportions peaked at 19% of 21-29 year-olds.

- The youngest and oldest age groups were more likely to be given a conditional or absolute discharge — 16% and 14% of under 18s and over 50s respectively, compared to 6% to 9% of other age groups.

Distribution of disposals for violent offences 1999

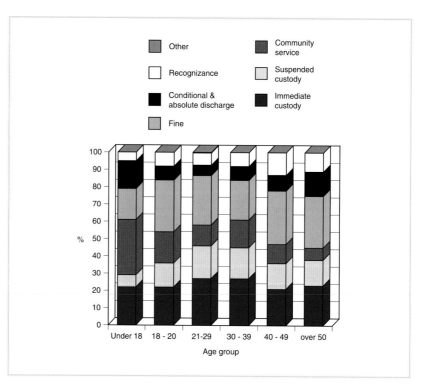

[1] Includes violence against the person, sexual offences and robbery.

Source: NIO Statistics and Research Branch

Disposals for acquisitive offences[1] 1999

- In 1999 community service was the disposal given most frequently to those convicted of acquisitive offences (27%), followed by immediate custody (24%) and fines (19%).

- Under 18s had the lowest chance of receiving a fine (10%) and the proportions receiving a fine generally increased with age to 33% of over 50s.

- Under 18s had the highest chance of receiving community service (42%) and the proportions generally decreased with age to 12% of over 50s.

- Immediate custody was a less likely disposal for those convicted of acquisitive offences if they were either under 18 (18%) or over 50 (12%) compared to 29% of both 18-20 year-olds and 21-29 year-olds.

- The proportion of under 18s given suspended custody (5%) was less than half the proportion of any other age group, which ranged from 14% of 18-20 year-olds to 19% of 21-29 year-olds.

- The youngest and oldest age groups were more likely to be conditionally or absolutely discharged than any of the other age groups — 24% of under 18 year-olds and 26% of over 50s, compared to 10% to 21% of other age groups.

Distribution of disposals for acquisitive offences 1999

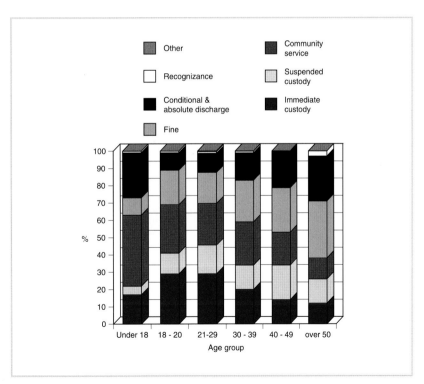

Source: NIO Statistics and Research Branch

[1] Includes theft, burglary and fraud and forgery.

Disposals for summary offences[1] 1999

- Overall, a fine was the most frequent sentence given to those convicted of summary offences (48%) in 1999 and recognizance was the second most frequent (23%).

- Under 18s (8%) and over 50s (6%) made up only a small proportion of those sentenced for summary offences.

- Under 18s had the lowest chance of being fined (26%) - approximately half the proportion of other age groups, which ranged from 46% of 30-39 year-olds to 51% of both 21-29 year-olds and over 50s.

- Community service was a considerably more likely disposal to be given to under 18s (24%) than to any other age group — 5% of over 50s to 8% of 21-29 year-olds.

- The proportion of under 18s given a conditional or absolute discharge (24%) was two to three times that for any other age group, which increased from 8% of 18-20 year-olds to 13% of over 50s.

Distribution of disposals for summary offences 1999

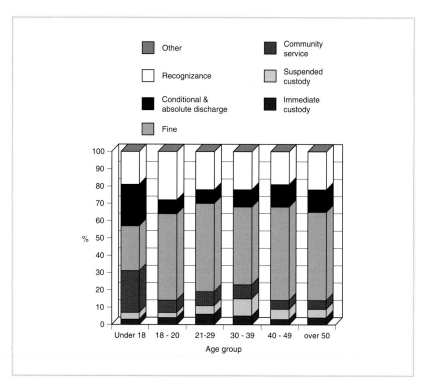

[1] Excludes all motoring offences.

Source: NIO Statistics and Research Branch

IMPRISONMENT

Chapter
8

Imprisonment

Summary

On an average day in 2001 in Northern Ireland s prisons there were around 350 prisoners aged 21-29 years, 250 aged 30-39 years, 100 aged 40-49 years and 50 aged 50-59 years. There were about 140 prisoners, on average, aged under 21 years and only around 13 aged 60 years or over.

Around one third of remand prisoners were aged 21-29 years old and almost 9 out of 10 were under 40 years old. Almost two thirds of fine default prisoners were under 30 years old and almost 9 out of 10 under 40 years old. On average, 1 in 10 sentenced prisoners was aged 17-20 and more than half in total were under 30 years old. Eight out of 10 sentenced prisoners were under 40 years old.

The age distribution of prison receptions shows a similar pattern to the average daily population described above. Just over one third of remand prisoners received were aged 21-29 years and almost 9 out of 10 were under 40 years old. Almost two thirds received for fine default were under 30 years old and just over 8 out of 10 were under 40 years old. Almost a quarter of prisoners received on sentence of immediate custody were under 21 years old, two thirds were under 30 and almost 9 out of 10 were under 40 years old.

Note: Age of prisoners refers to age at time of reception

Average population

- On an average day in Northern Ireland in 2001 there were 904[1] prisoners of which 266 (29%) were on remand, 616 (68%) sentenced and 22 (2%) fine defaulters.

- The greatest age-grouping within this population was 21-29 years (352), accounting for 39% of all prisoners. This is followed by 28% (253) within the age bracket 30-39 years. These combined age groups of 21-39 year-olds accounted for two thirds (67%) of the average NI prison population in 2001.

- The age range 14-16 years contributed to less than 0.5% (4) of the average daily prison population in 2001; 17-20 year-olds (138) represented 15%; 40-49 years (97) 11%; 50-59 years (49) 5%, and 60+ (13) 1%.

Average daily prison population 2001

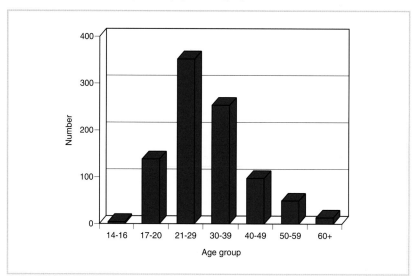

---

[1] Excludes non-criminal prisoners

Source: NIO Statistics and Research Branch

Average population by type of prisoner

- Of prisoners held on remand on an average day in 2001, the largest age group was 21-29 years (36%). The second largest age group was 30-39 years (28%) followed by 17-20 years (23%).

- Those prisoners held on remand between the ages of 14 and 16 and over the age of 59 together accounted for only 1% of all remand prisoners on an average day in 2001.

- On an average day, almost half (45%) of fine defaulters fell within the age range 21-29 years. No fine default prisoner was aged between 14-16 or 60+.

- On average, 40% of sentenced prisoners were aged 21-29. The second largest group was 30-39 year-olds (28%). Together sentenced prisoners aged 21-39 accounted for over two thirds (68%) of all sentenced prisoners.

- Young prisoners aged 14-16 made up less than 0.5% of all sentenced prisoners.

Average prison population by type of prisoner 2001

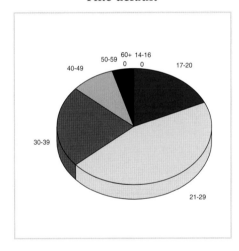

Remand   Fine default

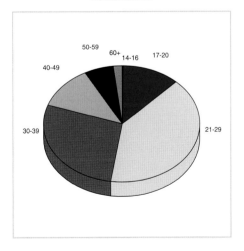

Sentenced

Source: NIO Statistics and Research Branch

Average remand population 2001 - Principal offence

- In 2001 there were, on an average day, 157 (60%) prisoners held on remand for violent offences (violence against the person, sexual offences and robbery); 50 (19%) for acquisitive offences (burglary, theft, fraud and forgery); and 55 (21%) for other offences (criminal damage, drug offences, motoring and other miscellaneous offences).

- Around two thirds of remand prisoners aged 21-29 (66%), 30-39 (60%) and over 40 years old (69%) were on remand for violent offences. This compares to under half (46%) of 14-20 year-olds.

- Remand prisoners aged 14-20 years-old (36%) were more likely than prisoners in older age groups to be on remand for acquisitive offences.

Average remand population by principal offence 2001

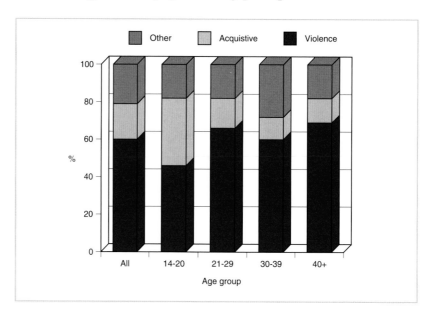

IMPRISONMENT

Average sentenced population 2001 - Principal offence

- On an average day in 2001 there were 387 (63%) sentenced (immediate custody) prisoners imprisoned for violent offences (violence against the person, sexual offences and robbery); 90 (15%) for acquisitive offences (burglary, theft, fraud and forgery); and 136 (22%) for other offences (criminal damage, drug offences, motoring and other miscellaneous offences).

- For all age groups, the most common offence type committed was violence. This likelihood increased with age, representing 47% of 14-20 year-olds, 61% of 21-29 year-olds, 66% of 30-39 year-olds and 74% of prisoners aged over 40 years old.

- The likelihood of being sentenced to imprisonment for an acquisitive offence on average decreased with age, representing 29% of 14-20 year-olds, 15% of 21-29 year-olds, 11% of 30-39 year-olds and 10% of prisoners aged over 40 years old.

Average sentenced (immediate custody) population by principal offence 2001

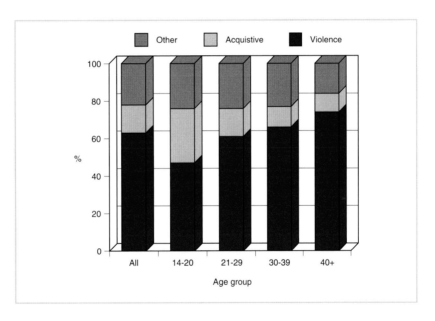

Source: NIO Statistics and Research Branch

69

Average sentenced population 1992-2001

- Through the period 1992-2001 there has been an overall reduction in the number of sentenced prisoners on an average day in NI. This number has more than halved (55%) from 1,362 prisoners in 1992 to 616 in 2001.

- This decrease is mainly due to the fall in prisoner numbers aged 17-39, the biggest age group in this population. The greatest drop in prisoner numbers was within the 21-29 age group, where numbers have consistently fallen from 732 in 1993 to 247 in 2001 — a fall of 66%.

- The greatest annual drop in prisoner numbers also occurred within the 21-29 age range between 1998-1999. This period saw a drop of 32% in this age group from 501 to 340 prisoners. Between these years the overall prison population fell by 260, of which 62% resulted through 21-29 year-olds.

- The age groups between 14-49 all experienced an overall decrease in prisoner numbers during the years 1992-2001. In contrast the average prison population aged 50 and above demonstrated an overall rise in prisoner numbers, despite annual fluctuation.

Average sentenced population 1992-2001

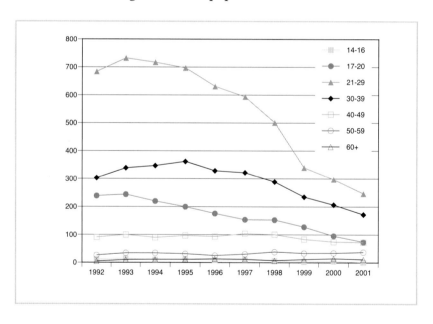

Source: NIO Statistics and Research Branch

Prison receptions

- Northern Ireland prison receptions in 2001 totalled 4,358[1], of which 1,922 (44%) were remand receptions; 1,393 (32%) fine default, and 1,043 (24%) sentenced prisoners.

- 37% (1,627) of all prison receptions in 2001 fell within the 21-29 age range; 26% (1,125) of receptions were aged 17-20, and 23% (987) aged 30-39.

- 86% (3,739) of all receptions in 2001 were aged between 17-39, with only a combined total of 2% (77) aged between 14-16 and 60+.

Prison receptions 2001

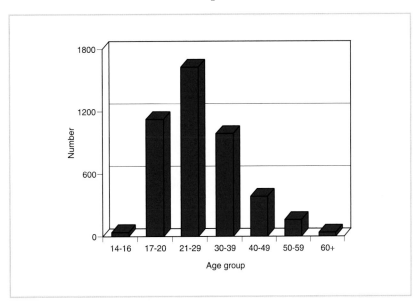

[1] Excludes non-criminal prisoners

Source: NIO Statistics and Research Branch

Prison receptions by type of prisoner

• Of prisoners received on remand in 2001, the largest age-grouping was 21-29 years, making up 35% (657) of this population. This was followed by 17-20 year-olds, who made up 30% (581) while 30-39 year-olds accounted for 22% (422).

• Prisoners aged between 14-16 (25) and 60+ (17) accounted for only 1% each of all remand receptions in 2001.

• The biggest age group within the 1,393 fine defaulters received in 2001 was 21-29 years (39%). Fine default receptions aged 14-16 accounted for less than 0.5% (6).

• 40% of sentenced (immediate custody) receptions in 2001 (421) were within the age range 21-29. 86% of all sentenced receptions in NI were aged between 17-39.

• Equal proportions (1%) of sentenced (immediate custody) prisoners aged 14-16 years old and over 60 years old were received into prison in 2001.

Prison receptions by type of prisoner 2001

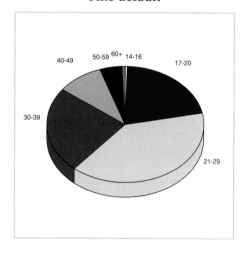

Sentenced (immediate custody)

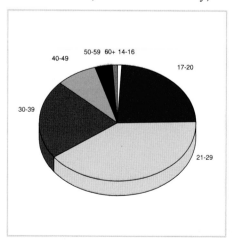

Source: NIO Statistics and Research Branch

Remand receptions 2001 - Principal offence

- In 2001 there were 869 (45%) remand receptions for violent offences (violence against the person, sexual offences and robbery); 536 (28%) for acquisitive offences (burglary, theft, fraud and forgery); and 517 (27%) for other offences (criminal damage, drug offences, motoring and other miscellaneous offences).

- Prisoners within the younger age group of 14-20 (45%) were most likely to be remanded for acquisitive offences. The likelihood of being remanded for an acquisitive crime declines with age, comprising 27% of 21-29 year-olds, 16% of 30-39 year-olds and 10% of those aged over 40.

- For those prisoners aged over 20, violent offences were the dominant cause of remand, accounting for almost half (47%) of 21-29 year-olds and more than half of 30-39 year-olds (53%) and those aged over 40 (51%).

Remand receptions by principal offence 2001

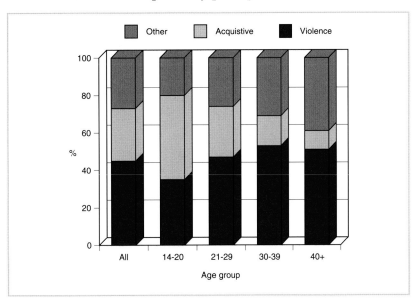

Sentenced receptions 2001 - Principal offence

- In 2001 there were 349 (33%) sentenced (immediate custody) receptions for violent offences (violence against the person, sexual offences and robbery); 309 (42%) for acquisitive offences (burglary, theft, fraud and forgery); and 385 (37%) for other offences (criminal damage, drug offences, motoring and other miscellaneous offences).

- Prisoners within the younger age group of 14-20 (42%) were most likely to enter prison for acquisitive offences. The likelihood of entering prison for an acquisitive crime declines with age, comprising 28% of 21-29 year-olds, 27% of 30-39 year-olds and 15% of those aged over 40.

- Prisoners aged 21-29 (39%) and 30-39 (39%) were most likely to be received into immediate custody for other offences. Prisoners aged over 40 (47%) were most likely to come into immediate custody for violent offences.

Sentenced (immediate custody) receptions by principal offence 2001

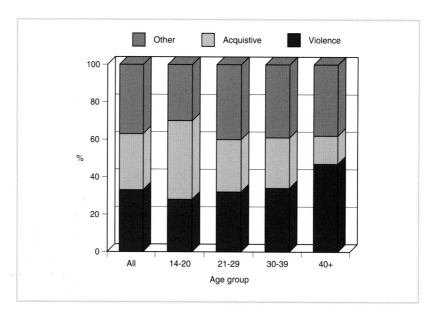

Source: NIO Statistics and Research Branch

Sentenced receptions 1992-2001

- Through the period 1992-2001 there was an overall reduction of 21% in the number of sentenced receptions in NI prisons. The greatest number of sentenced receptions during this period was in 1993 (1,551).

- Since 1992 the 21-29 age group has undergone the greatest numerical drop in prisoner numbers (180 or 30%), while proportionally the 14-16 age group has experienced the greatest drop (65% or 15 receptions).

- The largest annual drop in prisoner numbers again occurred within the 21-29 age group between 2000-2001, with a fall of 22% (122).

- An overall decline in receptions since 1992 occurred within the age range 14-29. In contrast, the prison population aged 30 and over has experienced an overall increase in number.

Sentenced receptions 1992-2001

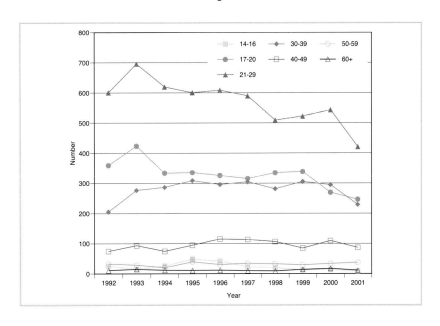

Source: NIO Statistics and Research Branch